My Book of
Gymnastics

Hello!

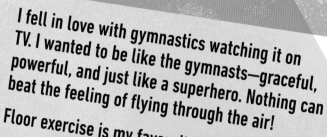

I fell in love with gymnastics watching it on TV. I wanted to be like the gymnasts—graceful, powerful, and just like a superhero. Nothing can beat the feeling of flying through the air!

Floor exercise is my favourite event, because we get to show our personality through our music and dance elements. I love being able to perfect a new skill, even if I have to practise it over and over again. There's almost an excitement after you fall, knowing you might nail it at the very next attempt.

I hope this book will inspire you, the way gymnastics inspired me. Never give up on chasing your dreams, no matter what they may be. You've got this!

Laurie Hernandez,
Olympic gold medallist

DK | Penguin Random House

Author and consultant Vincent Walduck

Senior editor Jolyon Goddard
Senior art editor Jim Green
Editorial assistant Katie Lawrence
Additional editorial Abby Aitcheson,
Seeta Parmar, Kathleen Teece, Becky Walsh
Illustrations Dan Crisp
DTP designer Vijay Kandwal
Project picture researcher Sakshi Saluja
Jacket co-ordinator Issy Walsh
Jacket designer Katie Knutton
Managing editors Laura Gilbert,
Jonathan Melmoth
Managing art editor Diane Peyton Jones
Assistant pre-producer Abi Maxwell
Senior producer Amy Knight
Creative directors Clare Baggaley,
Helen Senior
Publishing director Sarah Larter

First published in Great Britain in 2020
by Dorling Kindersley Limited
One Embassy Gardens, 8 Viaduct Gardens, London, SW11 7BW

Copyright © 2020 Dorling Kindersley Limited
A Penguin Random House Company
10 9 8 7 6 5 4 3
004–316626–May/2020

A CIP catalogue record for this book
is available from the British Library.
ISBN: 978-0-2414-1222-0

Printed and bound in China

A WORLD OF IDEAS:
SEE ALL THERE IS TO KNOW

www.dk.com

Contents

04 What is gymnastics?

06 Early gymnastics

08 Artistic gymnastics

10 Floor

12 Cartwheel backflip

14 Parallel bars

16 Asymmetric bars

18 Upstart

20 High bar

22 Still rings

24 Pommel horse

26 Scissor forward

28 Vault

30 Balance beam

32 Back walkover

34 Rhythmic gymnastics

36 Teamwork

38 Star gymnasts

40 Trampolining

42 Back somersault with full twist

44 Acrobatic gymnastics

46 Aerobic gymnastics

48 Parkour

50 Training

52 Scoring

54 Competitions

56 Facts and figures

58 Quiz

60 Glossary

62 Index

64 Acknowledgements

What is gymnastics?

Gymnastics covers a variety of sports, or disciplines. The most popular are **artistic gymnastics, rhythmic gymnastics,** and **trampolining**. All disciplines involve great skill, strength, flexibility, balance, and dance movements.

Aerobic gymnastics

This fast-paced sport developed out of the aerobics exercise craze. It requires speed and energy – and gives the heart and lungs a great workout.

Artistic gymnastics

Artistic gymnasts perform breathtaking routines on pieces of apparatus, such as the pommel horse and balance beam. They dazzle the world at the Summer Olympics every four years.

Did you know?

Many sports scientists believe that gymnastics is the most difficult sport to master.

4

Trampolining

Trampolinists perform acrobatic movements in the air, including twists and turns, while bouncing up to several metres high on a spring-bound bed. Along with artistic gymnastics and rhythmic gymnastics, trampolining is an Olympic sport.

Acrobatic gymnastics

In this sport, two or more gymnasts showcase their strength, balancing, and acrobatic skills, especially when creating spectacular human pyramids.

Rhythmic gymnastics

Highly skilled gymnasts perform a mixture of artistic gymnastics and ballet moves, while keeping a piece of apparatus, such as a ball or hoop, constantly moving.

Parkour

The gymnasts who perform parkour are called traceurs. They run, climb, swing, jump, vault, and somersault around, under, over, or through obstacles, usually in an urban setting.

This ancient painting of a bull-leaper decorates a wall in a Cretan palace.

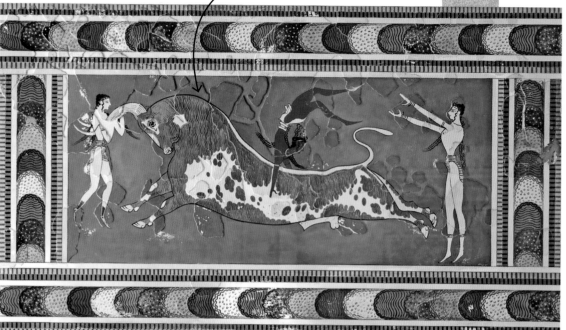

Minoan Crete

More than 3,000 years ago, the Minoan civilization flourished on the island of Crete, in the Mediterranean Sea. Young men would show off gymnastic skills and bravery by somersaulting over huge bulls.

Carved in stone, Egyptian dancers perform acrobatic moves.

Early gymnastics

People have performed gymnastics for thousands of years. In ancient times, acrobats took part in ceremonies or entertained onlookers. Soldiers practised gymnastic exercises to keep themselves fighting fit. In the late 18th century, gymnastics was included in the first modern Olympics.

Ancient Egypt

Acrobatic dancing often took place during festivals and ceremonies in ancient Egypt. Dancers would also entertain the pharaoh, or king, with their skilful moves.

e Olympic Games

e first modern Olympic Games
re held in Athens, Greece, in
96. Only men were allowed to
mpete. It wasn't until 1928
t the first female
mnasts competed
the Games.

A Danish woman
demonstrates
gymnastics in
London, in 1908.

Padding covers
the pommel horse.

Inspirational Olga

At the 1972 Olympics
in Munich, Germany,
17-year-old Soviet
gymnast **Olga Korbut**
won three gold medals.
She inspired children
around the world to
take up gymnastics.

Gymnasts performing
mallakhamb need to
have great strength.

Mallakhamb

A type of gymnastics called
mallakhamb has been practised
in India for hundreds of years.
Athletes perform yoga poses
and wrestling grips on top
of a pole, or while hanging
from a pole or rope.

Korbut won six
Olympic medals
in total – four golds
and two silvers.

7

Artistic gymnastics

This is the oldest type of gymnastics. Female gymnasts perform on four kinds of apparatus, and male gymnasts on six. Artistic gymnasts must have great body coordination and be dynamic, flexible, courageous, and calm under pressure.

It takes many hours of training to build up enough strength to master the rings.

Still rings

The male gymnasts who specialize in the still rings have exceptional strength. For this reason, they are generally not all-rounders. Their highly muscular bodies are not well suited to floor or swinging high bar routines.

Did you know?

Modern balance beams are made of aluminium covered in padding and artificial suede.

Balance beam

The riskiest apparatus for women is only 10 cm (4 in) wide. Doing moves on the beam requires an incredible sense of balance. While performing on the tightrope-like beam, gymnasts must keep their legs straight and toes pointed.

Laurie Hernandez's beam routine helped the US "Final Five" team win gold at the 2016 Olympics in Rio de Janeiro, Brazil.

Ring grips protect the gymnast's hands.

Gymnasts fly high between the two bars during their routines.

Key facts

- Women perform on vault, asymmetric bars, balance beam, and floor
- Men perform on floor, pommel horse, still rings, vault, parallel bars, and high bar
- Performed individually, but there are also team events

Asymmetric bars

After building up momentum, female gymnasts create exciting sequences of movements on the asymmetric, or uneven, bars. They swing in both directions, around the two bars, performing twists and somersaults while leaping between them.

Skin-coloured supports are worn to protect joints from injuries.

Flexibility is essential for the floor exercise and rewarded by judges.

Floor

The spectacle of the floor exercise makes it the showpiece event of artistic gymnastics. Routines include jaw-dropping tumbles and inventive moves within the confines of a square, springy floor. Women perform to music for up to 90 seconds, and men perform without music for up to 70 seconds.

Women's floor

The women's floor routine must include dance and acrobatics, including three to four complex tumbles. Captain of the Chinese women's team, **Liu Tingting** shows grace and elegance in this leap.

High-scoring moves

🏅 **Biles II** Double back somersault with three twists

🏅 **Shirai** Back somersault with four twists

🏅 **Podkopayeva** Double front somersault with half twist

Apparatus

The performance area of the square floor has sides measuring 12 m (39 ft). The floor is made of plywood covered in rubber foam, and may contain springs, too.

The floor has a safety border of 1 m (3.3 ft).

Did you know?

One hundred years ago, the floor area was sometimes made of woven coconut fibres!

Pointed toes are required when holding a position or in flight.

Men's floor

Japan's **Wataru Tanigawa** performs a V-sit move on the floor. Gymnasts should use the whole area during their routines. However, men mostly use the long diagonal lengths of the floor to get the most speed and height in their tumbles.

Wrists sometimes need supports to strengthen them as a lot of force is placed on them.

11

1 The cartwheel backflip begins with the first leg bent and the second leg straight. The hands come down towards the floor.

2 The second leg rises and the hands touch the floor. The first leg is straight and starts to push up off the floor.

The feet are pointed throughout this move.

3 The body twists, with the second leg now on the floor and the first leg in the air. The hands are on the floor but facing the opposite direction.

Double skill

The cartwheel backflip combines two commonly used moves in gymnastics: a cartwheel and a backflip. Top gymnasts can perform this effortlessly and with such speed that it is hard to tell where the cartwheel ends and the backflip begins!

Cartwheel backflip

4 Once both legs are on the floor, the arms come up above the head. The legs begin to bend and then push up off the floor.

5 The arms swing backwards over the head and the body is arched. The hands find the floor. The first leg kicks up over the head.

6 The second leg comes over the body. Both legs reach the floor and the arms are raised in the air. The cartwheel backflip is complete!

n a floor routine, gymnasts can use a move called a cartwheel backflip as part of one of their tumbles. This move begins facing one way and finishing n the opposite direction. It equires leg and arm strength.

MEDAL WINNER

Japanese gymnast **Mai Murakami** won gold in the floor event at the 2017 World Championships in Montréal, Canada.

13

Parallel bars

This male-only event combines strength, skill, and artistry. Gymnasts perform a series of swings and other moves between two bars of the same height a short distance apart. Routines use the whole length of the bars and last from 30 to 45 seconds.

Tippelt

US gymnast **Sam Mikulak** performs a difficult move called the Tippelt on the parallel bars. Routines mix swinging moves with held positions that show off a gymnast's strength.

High-scoring moves

🏅 **Zonderland** Like a Diamidov but with an extra back turn instead of a final handstand

🏅 **Bhavsar** Swinging move from one end of the bars to the other with a back straddle

🏅 **Kato dismount** Tucked double back with full twist

The bars are shap like long cylinders

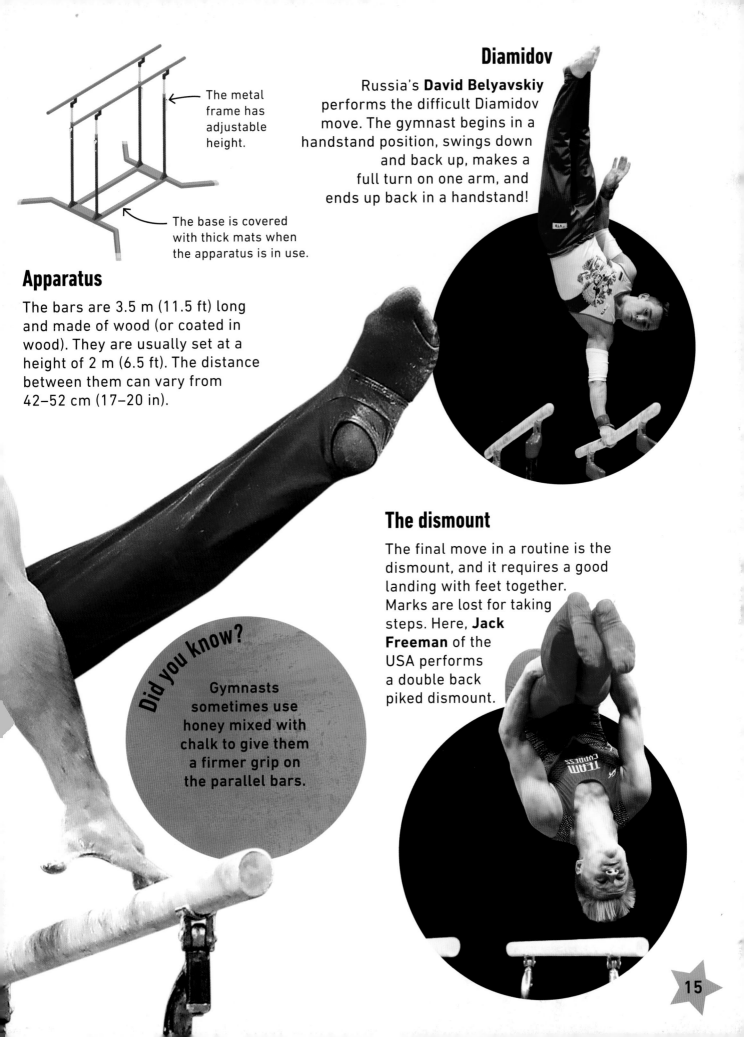

The metal frame has adjustable height.

The base is covered with thick mats when the apparatus is in use.

Apparatus

The bars are 3.5 m (11.5 ft) long and made of wood (or coated in wood). They are usually set at a height of 2 m (6.5 ft). The distance between them can vary from 42–52 cm (17–20 in).

Diamidov

Russia's **David Belyavskiy** performs the difficult Diamidov move. The gymnast begins in a handstand position, swings down and back up, makes a full turn on one arm, and ends up back in a handstand!

The dismount

The final move in a routine is the dismount, and it requires a good landing with feet together. Marks are lost for taking steps. Here, **Jack Freeman** of the USA performs a double back piked dismount.

Did you know?

Gymnasts sometimes use honey mixed with chalk to give them a firmer grip on the parallel bars.

15

Asymmetric bars

Also called the uneven bars, this women's event developed when female gymnasts used the parallel bars in a different way from the men. Routines last up to 45 seconds and include a series of swings, somersaults, and other moves on or between the two bars.

In flight

Here, US gymnast **Simone Biles** is leaping between the bars. Over the years, the distance between the bars has increased to let gymnasts do ever more daring and complicated mid-air moves.

The bars are made of fibreglass coated in wood.

Leather hand grips protect the gymnast's skin.

High-scoring moves

Tkachev Back giant circle releasing into a back straddle over the bar

Jaeger Front giant into a front somersault before catching the bar

Endo

Switzerland's **Lucia Tacchelli** is in a straddle position, in which the legs are wide apart. It is part of a circling move called the Endo.

Shaposh

This popular but difficult move, performed here by UK gymnast **Ellie Downie**, involves swinging around the low bar before releasing and flipping to catch the high bar.

The base is covered in safety mats when in use.

Cables keep the bars tense and tight.

Apparatus

Both bars are 2.4 m (7.9 ft) long. The high bar is usually 2.5 m (8.2 ft) from the floor and the low bar 1.7 m (5.6 ft). The distance between the bars can vary from 1.3–1.8 m (4.3–5.9 ft).

Using the higher bar

Gymnasts who start their asymmetric bars routine with an upstart use the high bar during this move. If they use the low bar, the move is called a float upstart and the legs need to be swung out of the way at the start, so they don't hit the floor.

2 The hands grip onto the high bar and the legs swing forwards.

3 The legs move into the pike position, and the hands are now behind the head.

1 The upstart begins with both legs pushing upwards off the springboard.

The back stays straight throughout this move.

Upstart

One way gymnasts begin their asymmetric bars routine is with a move called an upstart, or kip. This move is used on the higher of the two bars. Gymnasts need huge amounts of upper-body strength and perfect timing to perform an upstart successfully.

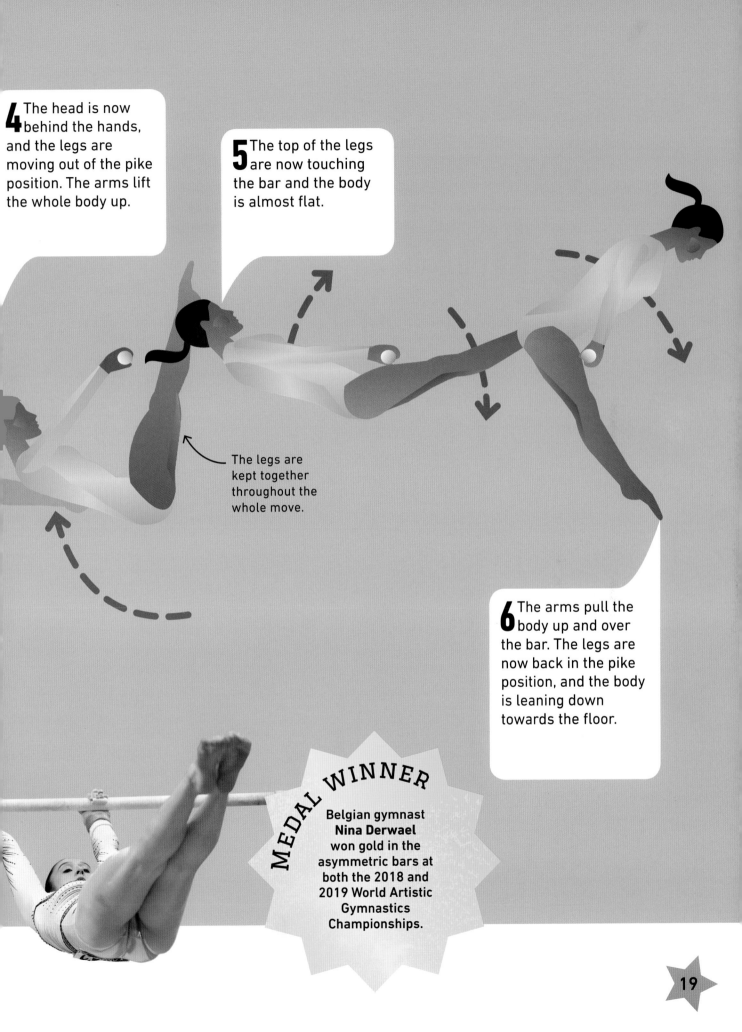

4 The head is now behind the hands, and the legs are moving out of the pike position. The arms lift the whole body up.

5 The top of the legs are now touching the bar and the body is almost flat.

The legs are kept together throughout the whole move.

6 The arms pull the body up and over the bar. The legs are now back in the pike position, and the body is leaning down towards the floor.

MEDAL WINNER

Belgian gymnast **Nina Derwael** won gold in the asymmetric bars at both the 2018 and 2019 World Artistic Gymnastics Championships.

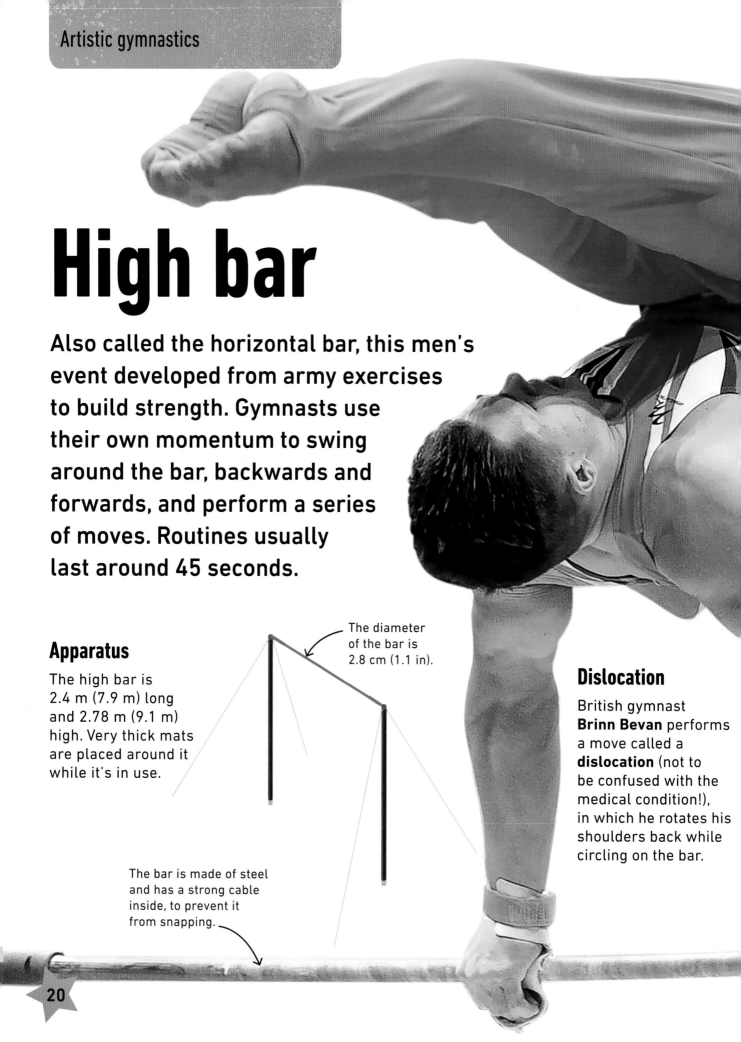

High bar

Also called the horizontal bar, this men's event developed from army exercises to build strength. Gymnasts use their own momentum to swing around the bar, backwards and forwards, and perform a series of moves. Routines usually last around 45 seconds.

Apparatus

The high bar is 2.4 m (7.9 m) long and 2.78 m (9.1 m) high. Very thick mats are placed around it while it's in use.

The diameter of the bar is 2.8 cm (1.1 in).

The bar is made of steel and has a strong cable inside, to prevent it from snapping.

Dislocation

British gymnast **Brinn Bevan** performs a move called a **dislocation** (not to be confused with the medical condition!), in which he rotates his shoulders back while circling on the bar.

Hand grips

Bar gymnasts protect their hands from sores and blisters. They wear hand grips that strap around their wrists. A leather part covers the palm and has holes for fingers to pass through.

The dismount

Gymnasts finish a high bar routine with a flourish of twists and somersaults. They need to land on two feet – losing balance and taking a step will reduce their score.

One-arm moves

Some moves on the high bar use one arm. American gymnast **Paul Hamm** performed a **one-armed giant** during his high bar routine at the 2004 Olympics in Athens, Greece. It helped him clinch the gold in the men's all-around event.

High-scoring moves

- **Kovács** Fast swinging into a double back somersault, and recatching the bar
- **Double-twisting Kovács** Kovács with an added double twist

21

Still rings

The still rings is a male-only event. It is one of the most difficult pieces of apparatus to master. It takes many years for boys to develop the muscles and core strength needed for the rings. Routines include a swing into a handstand, held positions, and a dismount.

Maltese cross

Japan's **Shogo Nonomura** performs an exceptionally difficult position called the Maltese cross. It is even harder to do if the gymnast swings into the position.

Legs are held straight to give elegant body lines.

Apparatus

The frame is 5.75 m (18.9 ft) high. The rings hang down to 2.75 m (9 ft) from the floor, and they are set 50 cm (1.6 ft) apart. The inner diameter of the rings is 18 cm (7.1 in). Thick mats are placed around the frame when it's in use.

High-scoring moves

⭐ **Guczoghy** Double back somersault without release of the rings

⭐ **Yamawaki** Double front somersault without release of the rings

⭐ **Tulloch** "Lying" position with the back facing the floor and the rings held out to the sides of the body

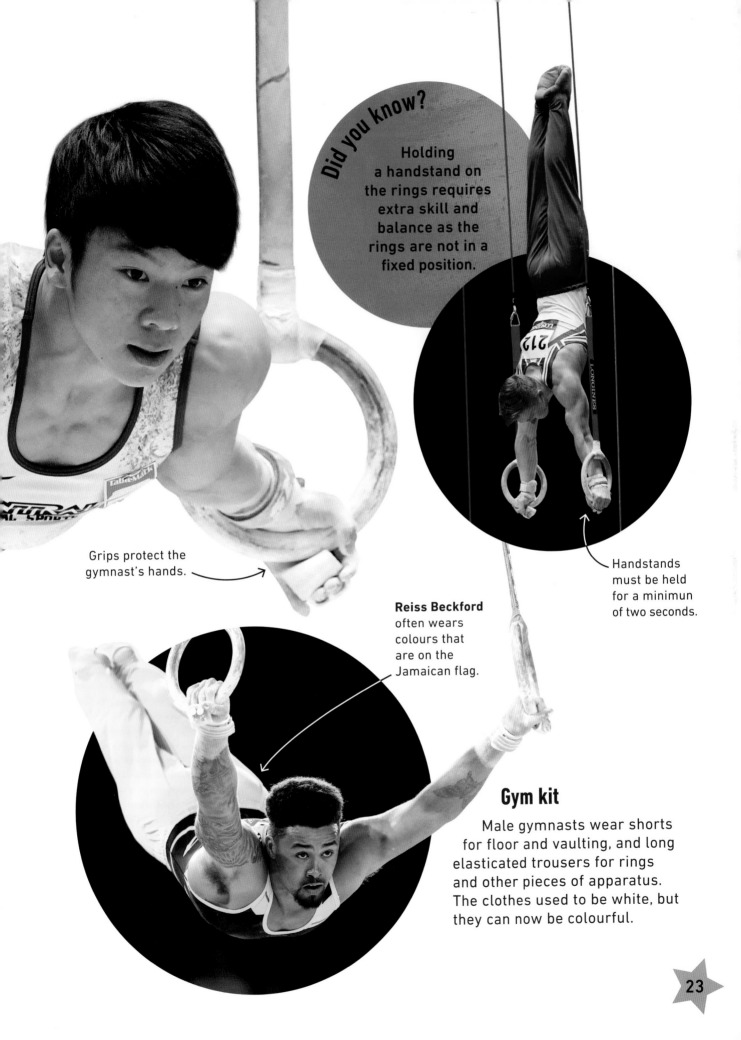

Did you know?

Holding a handstand on the rings requires extra skill and balance as the rings are not in a fixed position.

Grips protect the gymnast's hands.

Handstands must be held for a minimun of two seconds.

Reiss Beckford often wears colours that are on the Jamaican flag.

Gym kit

Male gymnasts wear shorts for floor and vaulting, and long elasticated trousers for rings and other pieces of apparatus. The clothes used to be white, but they can now be colourful.

Lots of arm strength is required for the pommel horse, a male-only event. Gymnasts hold onto the top of the pommel apparatus as they swing their legs around, above, and across the horse. The legs shouldn't touch the horse, which makes it even trickier!

Pommel horse

Did you know? Pommel horses were first used by soldiers who fought on horseback, to practise getting on and off their horses.

High-scoring moves

Magyar walk Circling while "walking" from one end of the horse to the other

Spindle Full body turn while circling

Busnari Flairs up to a handstand pirouette and back down into flair circles

Stretched legs and pointed toes are important.

Gymnasts might hold just one of the handles to turn during circling.

Single-leg section

UK gymnast **Louis Smith** swings his leg high into the air during the single-leg section of his routine.

Mushroom

Young gymnasts learn to circle with junior apparatus. Mushrooms were given their name because of their mushroom-like round tops. Boys use the apparatus to learn to extend their legs while they swing.

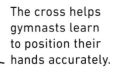

The cross helps gymnasts learn to position their hands accurately.

Leg skills

The legs are swung in a circle above the horse to perform the **circling** move. To make this move more flashy, the gymnast can use a wide split-leg position called a **flair**.

Gymnasts can hold onto the edges to "walk" along the horse.

Apparatus

The padded, leather-covered top of the pommel horse is 1.6 m (5.2 ft) long and stands 1.15 m (3.8 ft) high. The two wooden handles are around 45 cm (18 in) apart, but are adjustable to shoulder width.

Strong wrists are needed to perform on the pommel horse.

25

3 The leading leg comes down over the horse, and the hand returns to the pommel.

1 The scissor forward begins with both legs on one side of the horse.

2 The leading leg rises. The hand on that side comes away from the pommel (handle).

Scissor forward

In a pommel horse routine, gymnasts can use a move called a scissor forward to switch the position of the legs when they are on either side of the apparatus. This move needs a lot of upper-body strength and flexibility.

Single-leg skill

The scissor forward is a "single-leg" skill, where the legs move separately. Most of a routine uses "double-leg" skills, with the legs moving together.

4 The legs now swing upwards. The other arm comes away from the pommel, and the legs switch positions mid-air.

5 The legs come down either side of the horse, now in a switched position. The hand returns to the pommel. This move often leads into a handstand.

Vault

Both female and male gymnasts do this high-speed event. They sprint along a track and use a springboard to launch into a jump. They then push off the vault with their hands and soar high into the air, making mind-boggling moves before landing. This explosive event is over in just a few seconds.

Runway speed

Gymnasts need to sprint down the 25 m (82 ft) runway as fast as they can. This speed lets them vault high and far, but it needs to be controlled, so that they can perform tricky moves in the air.

Forward entry

Canadian **Ellie Black** is doing a **forward entry vault**. She has leapt forwards from the springboard straight onto the vault. Another type of vault is a **Tsukahara**, in which a gymnast performs a cartwheel or **round off** onto the vault.

Gymnasts can put their hands in different positions on the surface of the vault.

GVA

Apparatus

The vault is 1.2 m (3.9 ft) long and 95 cm (3.1 ft) wide. It is set at a height of 1.25 m (4.1 ft) for female gymnasts and 1.35 m (4.4 ft) for male gymnasts. It has a springboard in front and a thick mat behind it for landing.

Arms and shoulders need to be very strong, so that gymnasts can push off from the vault and fly high.

The height of the vault can be adjusted.

High-scoring moves

 Amanar Straight Yurchenko with two-and-a-half twists

 Drăgulescu Double front somersault with half turn

Yurchenko vault

This style of vault involves performing a round off at the end of the run-up to land on the springboard backwards. The gymnast then springs onto the vault in a backflip and pushes off into the air.

This gymnast has just done a backflip from the springboard.

High-flying moves

Gymnasts can make many mid-air moves when vaulting. German gymnast **Andreas Bretschneider** is doing a **somersault**. After spinning through the air, gymnasts must land on the mat with both feet together.

Gymnasts need strong leg muscles to jump high and stay balanced.

Balancing act

To excel on the beam, gymnasts need to be quick on their feet and have a great awareness of their surroundings. One wrong step when performing a difficult trick can bring a routine to a halt. Chinese gymnast **Zhang Jin** has style and treads lightly on the beam.

Did you know?

Gymnasts must travel back and forth along the whole length of the beam during their routines.

Balance beam

Female gymnasts compete on the balance beam. They perform routines, which last about 90 seconds, and have to do incredibly precise moves without falling off. They are judged on the difficulty and execution of their moves, as well as their dismount.

Double-double dismount

Many people think that American **Simone Biles** is the best gymnast the world has ever seen. She does the most difficult dismount on the balance beam – the double-double. Simone does two backflips on the beam to build up speed, before jumping into two twisting somersaults and then landing on two feet!

Simone performs a backflip during her double-double dismount from the beam.

High-scoring moves

🎖 **Yang Bo** Jump in which the legs are oversplit and the head is back

🎖 **Korbut** Backflip landing on the beam in a straddle position

The balance beam is made of wood with a soft covering.

Apparatus

The balance beam requires a lot of bravery and precision. It is 5 m (16.4 ft) long, 1.25 m (4.1 ft) high, and only 10 cm (4 in) wide, so falling off it during a routine is a risk. Mats are placed around the beam for protection.

Learn on the floor

Before attempting this difficult move on a balance beam, young gymnasts often first learn how to do it on the floor.

1 The move begins by raising the arms above the head. At the same time, the leading leg is raised and stretched out straight.

2 The body bends over backwards, while keeping the leading leg straight. The palms of the hands land on the beam. Weight is repositioned over the hands.

3 The body moves into a handstand with the legs in the splits position. The arms are straight.

Toes are pointed as the leg is raised.

Back walkover

4 The body moves into the landing position. The leading leg is straight as it touches down.

Trailing leg follows in a fluid motion.

Leading leg touches down first.

5 The move finishes with one leg raised in an arabesque position. Both arms are raised.

n this move, the gymnast makes a 360-degree backwards rotation. t showcases strength, flexibility, and superb balance, especially when performed on the balance beam.

Rhythmic gymnastics

In rhythmic gymnastics, competitors use dance and pieces of apparatus, such as a ribbon or hoop, to create dazzling routines. Rhythmic gymnastics events have been a part of the Summer Olympic Games since 1984.

Did you know?

Clubs are the most difficult apparatus to perform with because gymnasts need to use both hands constantly to hold them.

Ribbon routine

Kazakhstan's **Alina Adilkhanova** performs her ribbon routine. During this event, the ribbon must always be moving.

Rhythmic gymnastics includes dance moves, especially from ballet. Gymnasts must be flexible and have excellent balance.

Clubs

Rope

Hoop

Ball

Apparatus

The five types of apparatus used in rhythmic gymnastics are the rope, ribbon, ball, hoop, and clubs. The ceiling must be at least 8 m (26.2 ft) above the floor, so gymnasts can throw apparatus as high as possible.

The performance area is 13 x 13 m (42.7 x 42.7 ft).

Ribbon

Key facts

- For both men and women, but only women compete in the Olympics

- Each competition uses four out of the five pieces of apparatus

- The four pieces of apparatus used vary from competition to competition

Teamwork

Did you know?

Gymnasts throw pieces of apparatus to each other in a rhythmic routine. Throws have to be precise or the objects might collide mid-air!

Parts of the group routine are synchronized – they must be performed at the same time by all the gymnasts.

The ball weighs 400 g (14 oz).

Group routines are very important in rhythmic gymnastics. They include elements of dance and require perfect coordination. Teams must work together to deliver a spectacular performance, and each member is crucial to the whole team's success.

Group routines

In the rhythmic team event, gymnasts perform two routines: one with the same piece of apparatus and one with a mix, such as a hoop and a ball. In both types of routine, teamwork is key.

Artistic teams

Teams of artistic gymnasts do not perform together, they compete in individual events. All scores are added together, and a team's position in a competition is decided by the total.

A rhythmic gymnast's hoop is made of wood or plastic.

Support

As well as performing together, teammates are there to support each other – they win and lose together. Teammates give the best support as they are going through the exact same things at the same time.

Kōhei Uchimura

Considered by many to be the greatest ever male gymnast, Japan's Kōhei Uchimura won gold in the men's artistic individual all-around competition in both the 2012 and 2016 Olympics.

Simone Biles

Star of the 2016 Olympics, Simone Biles of the USA won five medals, four of which were golds. She also holds the all-time record for the most medals won at the World Championships.

Star gymnasts

Gymnasts who compete at Olympic or World Championship level are all amazing athletes. However, some are true stars. Their natural flair, focus, and dedication help them outshine their rivals and achieve record-breaking scores.

Champions have superb upper-body strength.

Rhythmic gymnastics mixes gymnastics and dance, and the use of apparatus.

Nadia Comăneci

At just 14, this gymnast from Romania became world famous when she was given a perfect score of 10 out of 10 at the 1976 Olympics in Montréal.

Alina Kabaeva

This Russian rhythmic gymnast won gold in the all-around competition in the 2004 Olympics in Athens.

Svetlana Khorkina

Russian multi-medallist Svetlana Khorkina has nine skills, or gymnastic moves, named after her. She competed at the 1996, 2000, and 2004 Olympics.

Nadia's powerful physique helped her win nine Olympic medals.

Epke Zonderland

This Dutch gymnast won gold on the horizontal bar at the 2012 Olympics in London. Nicknamed "The Flying Dutchman", Epke was the first Dutch gymnast to win an Olympic medal in an individual event.

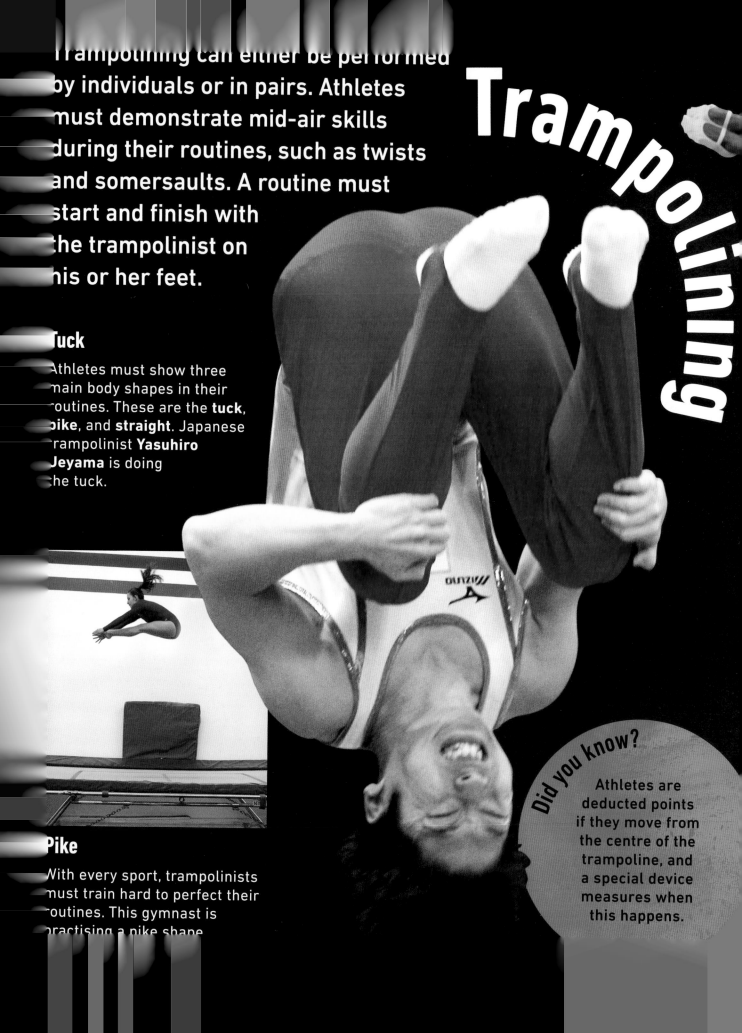

Trampolining can either be performed by individuals or in pairs. Athletes must demonstrate mid-air skills during their routines, such as twists and somersaults. A routine must start and finish with the trampolinist on his or her feet.

Tuck

Athletes must show three main body shapes in their routines. These are the **tuck**, **pike**, and **straight**. Japanese trampolinist **Yasuhiro Ueyama** is doing the tuck.

Trampolining

Pike

With every sport, trampolinists must train hard to perfect their routines. This gymnast is practising a pike shape.

Did you know?

Athletes are deducted points if they move from the centre of the trampoline, and a special device measures when this happens.

Pairs

Trampolinists performing in pairs must be **synchronized**. The two gymnasts must do the same moves at exactly the same time as each other. Their trampolines are placed side by side.

A red cross marks the centre of the trampoline.

Key Facts

- This event is for both male and female athletes

- Trampolinists can jump over 5 m (16.4 ft) high – higher than a double-decker bus!

- Athletes only have about two seconds to complete each move

Trampoline apparatus

Invented in 1936, the trampoline needs to be strong and steady for gymnasts to perform their moves. Trampolines have a metal frame, and safety mats at either end. The central jumping zone is 2.15 x 1.08 m (7 x 3.5 ft).

Tumbling

Trampolining competitions include tumbling events, too. Tumblers make their way down the tumble track by performing increasingly difficult and faster moves, such as back somersaults, as they go. The routine needs to be controlled well, as the athlete has to finish with a steady landing.

Tumble track apparatus

The tumble track is 25 m (82 ft) long and has a soft landing zone at the end. The track is sprung, which helps tumblers achieve the height they need to perform advanced moves.

Back somersault with full twist

Trampolinists can do a number of somersaults during their routine, but they must first master the basics. In the back somersault with full twist, their entire body twists in the air and they land facing the same way in which they started.

Keep twisting

As well as a full twist, trampolinists can do a half twist, or twist up to four times! They can also perform multiple somersaults in a tight tuck or piked shape, so the trampolinist spins faster. The more twists and somersaults they complete, the higher their score.

3 The body rotates to face the trampoline, while the arms can be tucked in to add more spin to the twist.

The abdominals are tightened to keep the body straight.

1 The twist begins close to the trampoline bed, after a few jumps to gain height. The arms and legs are extended and the feet and toes are pointed.

2 As the body continues to lean back, it starts to twist the 360 degrees of a full turn. All gymnasts have a preference to twist to the left or the right.

With feet pointed, the upper body tilts back.

4 The body turns upside down and twists to face backwards. The arms remain close to the body.

5 While falling back down, the body continues to twist, facing down towards the trampoline.

6 When the twist is complete, the arms begin to reach upwards in preparation for the landing.

Trampolinists need to look down to see how far away they are from the trampoline.

Landing the jump

To gain a higher score, trampolinists must land in the same spot they began their back somersault. If they travel (land away from their starting spot), they lose marks.

7 To return to the trampoline, the body finishes in a straight line with the arms lowering, ready for the next move.

43

Acrobatic gymnastics

The lightest acrobat is usually at the top.

Acrobatic gymnasts, or acrobats, compete in female, male, or mixed teams. This type of gymnastics requires balance and strength to do tricky moves with flair and style. Routines can last up to two-and-a-half minutes.

The wooden floor is carpeted and sprung, which makes it bouncy.

Strength

A crucial skill in acrobatic gymnastics is strength. Without it, acrobats in a team wouldn't be able to hold each other up to perform balancing acts, or do somersaults and tumbles!

Apparatus

The only apparatus used in acrobatic gymnastics is the **floor**. It's a perfect square, with each side measuring 12 m (39 ft) long. A safety border of 1m (3.3 ft) surrounds the performance area.

Gymnasts at the top have strong wrists to help them keep steady and balanced.

Balance

To perform acrobatic moves, such as a **human pyramid**, gymnasts need an incredible amount of balance. If one acrobat in the pyramid is not steady, the whole team can come crashing down.

Gymnasts at the base must have strong leg muscles to hold the weight of the gymnasts on top of them.

Dance

Music and dance are important in acrobatic gymnastics. Teams perform routines to music and are awarded points for choreography and style. Acrobats must engage with the judges and show good facial expressions to score extra points.

Aerobic gymnastics

A popular way to keep fit in the 1980s, aerobics is now a competitive sport. Aerobic gymnasts perform high-energy routines to music that last exactly one-and-a-half minutes and show off their flexibility, balance, and strength.

Pairs

Aerobic pairs are always made up of a man and a woman. Much of their routine needs to be synchronized, and it also has to include lifts.

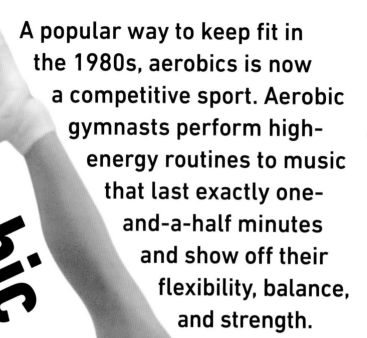

Routines are fast and packed with moves, so aerobic gymnasts need to be extremely fit.

Did you know?

An aerobic routine needs to be **non-stop**, so gymnasts have to be moving all the time.

Code of Points

Aerobic routines are performed to upbeat music. Gymnasts must do a variety of moves in their routines, which are listed in a rule book called the Code of Points. Important moves include high kicks and jumps.

46

Apparatus

Gymnasts use a sprung floor. Young gymnasts perform in the smaller square, with sides of 7 m (23 ft). Older performers and groups have more space and perform in the bigger square, with sides of 10 m (33 ft).

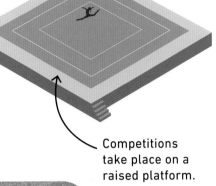

Competitions take place on a raised platform.

Key facts

- Both men and women compete in aerobic gymnastics
- Not yet an Olympic sport, but it has Continental and World Championships
- Gymnasts perform alone, in pairs, trios, or groups of five

Thai gymnast **Chanawit Thongdee** is holding a static strength move.

Gymnasts wear special shoes, which help them grip the floor.

Static strength

Moves in which gymnasts balance on their hands and stay completely still are known as static strength moves. They require a huge amount of upper-body strength.

47

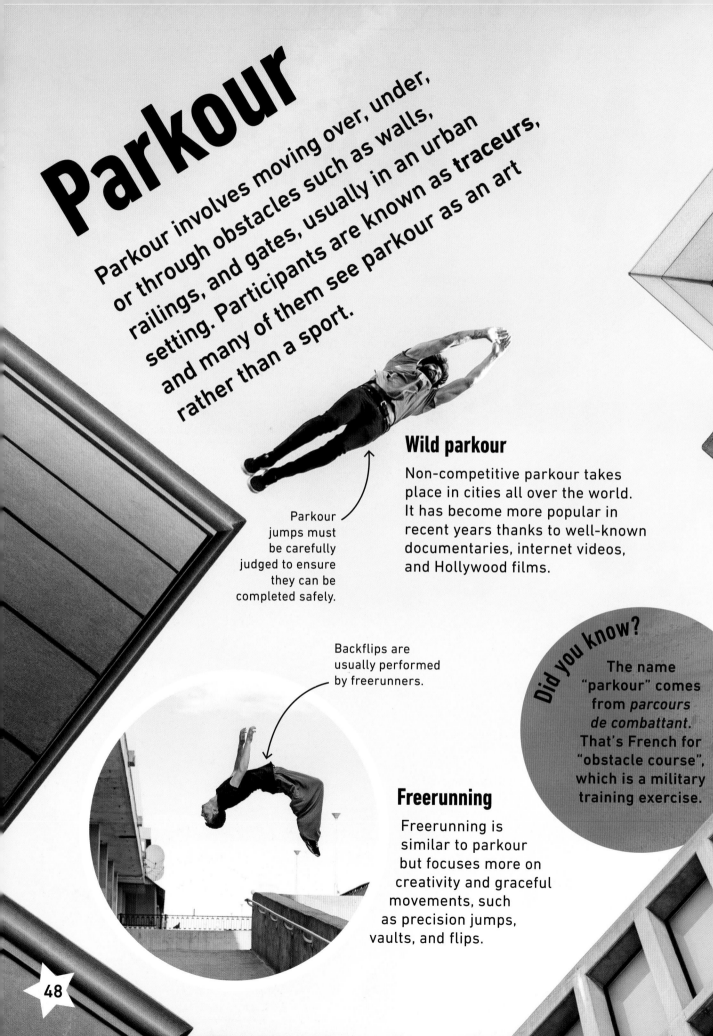

Parkour

Parkour involves moving over, under, or through obstacles such as walls, railings, and gates, usually in an urban setting. Participants are known as **traceurs**, and many of them see parkour as an art rather than a sport.

Parkour jumps must be carefully judged to ensure they can be completed safely.

Wild parkour

Non-competitive parkour takes place in cities all over the world. It has become more popular in recent years thanks to well-known documentaries, internet videos, and Hollywood films.

Backflips are usually performed by freerunners.

Did you know?

The name "parkour" comes from *parcours de combattant*. That's French for "obstacle course", which is a military training exercise.

Freerunning

Freerunning is similar to parkour but focuses more on creativity and graceful movements, such as precision jumps, vaults, and flips.

Parkour World Cup

The first FIG Parkour World Cup was held as part of the 2018 FISE World Action Sports Festival in Hiroshima, Japan. It took place on a 40 m (131 ft) course, and more than 30 athletes took part, representing 20 nations.

Only practise parkour moves under the supervision of experienced coaches or traceurs.

The Yamakasi

The first group of traceurs was known as the Yamasaki. The nine founding members came from Lisses, France, and included David Belle and **Sébastien Foucan**.

Key facts

- The term "parkour" was coined by David Belle in 1998
- In 2016, the United Kingdom was the first country to officially recognize parkour as a sport
- Practitioners associate parkour with mental discipline, dedication, and discovery

Training

To be a great gymnast, you have to train. If gymnasts are not confident with a move or a routine, they can end up hurting themselves. Many world-class gymnasts train at top gyms twice a day, seven days a week, to learn new skills and prepare for competitions.

In the gym

Good gyms have all the pieces of apparatus that gymnasts use in competitions. This equipment is often packed into a tight space, with most gyms being 30 x 30 m (98 x 98 ft) or smaller.

Did you know?

Most professional gymnastics gyms have **foam pits**. These soft landing areas allow gymnasts to learn new skills safely.

Coaching

Gymnasts and their coaches spend many hours together in training and competitions. Their relationship is very important, as the coach not only helps the gymnast improve skills, but also offers emotional and psychological support.

Russian gymnast **Angelina Melnikova** celebrates with one of her coaches.

American college system

Some American universities (or colleges) give scholarships to talented gymnasts. This means that the gymnasts pay less or, in some cases, receive free tuition, in return for competing for the college team.

Broccoli is a good source of fibre and vitamins.

Diet

When it comes to food, gymnasts must stick to a strict diet. They cannot have junk food, and must eat as healthily as possible to fuel their bodies when they train and perform.

Bananas are rich in minerals that gymnasts need, such as potassium.

Fish provides protein, which is good for building muscles.

Psychology

To be the best, gymnasts have to be very brave. Almost all of gymnastics can be dangerous, and athletes need to be prepared mentally, as well as physically, to overcome fear when attempting new skills and events.

51

Scoring

Gymnastics events aren't like most other sporting events in which there are clear winners, such as the team that scores the most goals. Gymnastics is half a sport and half an art form. Its routines are marked by panels of judges, and an average is taken to get the final score.

Judges marking

A panel of judges looks at different aspects of routines, including difficulty, execution, and artistry. One judge oversees the others, and computers may be used to check that the judges' scores are fair. These judges are marking a synchronized trampolining routine.

Who sets the rules?

The rules and scoring of almost all types of gymnastics are laid down by the Fédération Internationale de Gymnastique, or the FIG, which has its headquarters in Switzerland. **Morinari Watanabe** is the current president of the FIG.

No more perfect 10s

Gymnastics' marking system was changed in 2006. Scores can now be more than 10, but perfect scores are now impossible. **Lavinia Miloşovici** of Romania was the last gymnast to get a perfect score of 10, at the 1992 Olympics in Barcelona.

Furious people protested until Nemov was given a better mark.

Rescored!

Russian gymnast **Alexei Nemov** scored 9.725 for his high bar routine at the 2004 Olympics in Athens, but it was changed to 9.762 after angry protests from the crowd. Nemov himself tried to calm the crowd.

Gymnastics discipline	Number of judges		
	Difficulty	Artistic	Execution
Artistic	2	0	4 or 5
Rhythmic	2	4	4
Trampolining	2	0	4 or 5
Acrobatic	2	4	4
Aerobic	2	4	4

Different scores

Disciplines are scored differently, according to FIG guidelines. The number and types of judges vary. The figures in this table are based on major competitions, such as the Olympics. There may also be reference judges and a jury of appeal.

53

Competitions

Once gymnasts have done enough training, they can show off their skills at competitions. Starting at a local level, gymnasts work their way up to competing on the international stage. The most important competitions are the World Championships and the Olympics.

In the arena

Female and male events require different types of apparatus. Some big arenas can fit in all the apparatuses, but in most competitions it is changed overnight, and men and women compete on different days.

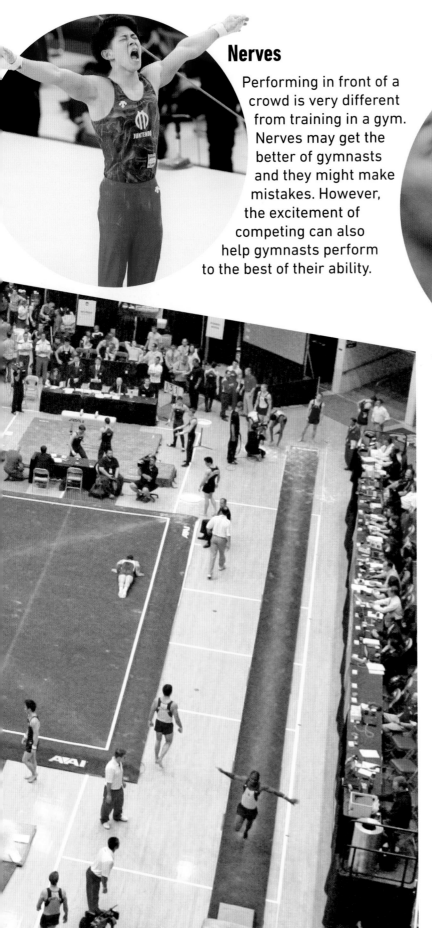

Nerves

Performing in front of a crowd is very different from training in a gym. Nerves may get the better of gymnasts and they might make mistakes. However, the excitement of competing can also help gymnasts perform to the best of their ability.

Waiting

A gymnastics competition usually lasts a couple of hours. When they're not performing, gymnasts have to wait patiently for their scores, and then for their next event. It's important to stay focused throughout.

Medals

Gymnasts gain valuable experience when competing, but also win medals. Here, **Epke Zonderland**, **Kōhei Uchimura**, and **Sam Mikulak** show off their gold, silver, and bronze medals for the high bar.

When Romania's **Nadia Comăneci** became the first Olympic gymnast to earn a "perfect 10" at the 1976 Olympics, the scoreboard wasn't able to display a score higher than 9.99. Her score was shown as 1.00 instead!

The close-fitting, stretchy garment worn by gymnasts is called a leotard. It is named after the 19th-century French acrobat **Jules Léotard,** who first made it popular.

Facts and figures

Here are some fascinating facts and figures from the amazing world of gymnastics.

Being short is an advantage in gymnastics. **Simone Biles** is only 1.42 m (4 ft 8 in) tall.

Russian gymnast **Aleksandr Dityatin** won eight medals at the **1980 Olympics in Moscow** (three gold, four silver, and one bronze). This is the joint-most medals won in any sport at a single Olympics.

56

The **music** used in women's artistic gymnastics floor routines is **not allowed** to feature spoken words or sung lyrics of any kind.

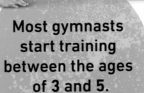

Most gymnasts start training between the ages of 3 and 5.

The medals awarded at the 2019 World Artistic Gymnastics Championships **glow when warmed up!**

The **medal ceremony** for the all-around title at the 2014 World Artistic Gymnastics Championships in Nanning, China, was briefly **disrupted by a bee**, which flew out of gold medallist Simone Biles's bouquet of flowers.

South African gymnast **Zama Mofokeng** holds the record for the most consecutive one-handed backflips. He did **34 in a row!**

Twins **Paul** and **Morgan Hamm** competed as part of Team USA in the 2004 Olympics in Athens, Greece.

German gymnast **Johanna Quaas** was born in **1925** and is still performing routines in her **90s.**

Quiz

Answers on page 64

1. What are the four artistic gymnastics events that women compete in?

A. Balance beam, parallel bars, floor, trampoline
B. Vault, asymmetric bars, balance beam, floor
C. Vault, balance beam, floor, ceiling
D. Vault, asymmetric bars, balance beam, javelin

2. What is the organization that governs, or sets the rules of, gymnastics commonly known as?

A. The DATE
B. The LIME
C. The FIG
D. The PLUM

3. What are the five pieces of apparatus used by rhythmic gymnasts?

A. Ball, clubs, hoop, ribbon, rope
B. Ball, clubs, flag, ribbon, stick
C. Ball, bat, yo-yo, hoop, ribbon
D. Beach ball, clubs, flag, hoop, rope

4. What are the medals awarded at the Olympic Games and World Gymnastics Championships?

A. Platinum, gold, silver
B. Gold, silver, bronze
C. Gold, silver, plastic
D. Diamond, gold, iron

5. Which artistic gymnast is known as the "Flying Dutchman" because of his amazing skills on the high bar?

A. Max Wunderleg
B. Epke Zonderland
C. Mike Londonland
D. Alex Wonderland

6. How wide is the balance beam?

7. Which kind of gymnastics was inspired by army obstacle courses?

8. What might a young gymnast use a "mushroom" for?

9. How often are the Summer Olympic Games held?

10. In which kind of gymnastics might you see a human pyramid?

11. Who were the "Final Five"?

12. When was the trampoline invented?

13. Who is known as the "father of gymnastics"?

14. In which artistic men's event might you see a gymnast perform the Diamidov?

DDR

35

59

Glossary

abdominals

Set of muscles that are in front of the stomach

acrobatic gymnastics

Type of gymnastics that includes balance work in pairs, trios, and fours

aerobic gymnastics

Type of gymnastics that involves fast-paced moves

all-around

Where gymnasts compete in all events during a competition

apparatus

Piece of equipment on which gymnasts perform, such as the vault or balance beam, or which rhythmic gymnasts use, such as the ball or hoop

arabesque

Position in which a gymnast stands on one leg, with the other leg extended out behind the body. Both legs should be straight

arena
Area in which gymnasts perform during competitions

artistic gymnastics

Type of gymnastics in which gymnasts perform routines on different types of apparatus, such as the floor

back

When a move is performed that requires a gymnast to jump backwards, such as a back somersault

choreography

Putting dance and gymnastic moves together to make a routine

circling

Move in which the legs are swung around in a circular motion, such as above the pommel horse

coordination

Moving different body parts at the same time

disciplines

Different types of gymnastics, such as artistic gymnastics, trampolining, and parkour

dislocation

Move in which a gymnast rotates the shoulders backwards while circling on the high bar

dismount

Move used to get off a piece of apparatus

FIG

Fédération Internationale de Gymnastique, the international organization that governs gymnastics

flair

Move in which the gymnast's legs are split wide while circling on the pommel horse

flexibility

Ability to bend freely

freerunning

Physical activity similar to parkour but focusing more on gymnastic movements, such as flips

front

When a move is perfomed that requires a gymnast to jump forwards, such as a front somersault

grips

Pieces of leather worn by gymnasts to improve grip, and protect the skin on their hands from blistering while performing and practising

Olympic Games

International sports competition, which is held every four years

parkour

Physical activity that involves moving over, under, or through obstacles, usually in a city setting

physique

Shape and size of the body

pike

Position in which the body and legs form a V-shape, as the legs are raised high and straight

pirouette

Spin or turn that may be done on the hands or feet

proteins

Nutrients that help your body build muscle and repair itself. Foods rich in protein include meat, fish, eggs, and cheese

rhythmic gymnastics

Form of gymnastics in which gymnasts perform routines that combine dance and gymnastics, while using handheld apparatus

round off

Move that is similar to a cartwheel, but gymnasts land on both feet at the same time

routine

Exercise made up of many moves performed by a gymnast to show a full range of skills

safety border

Area or zone that surrounds the performance area of the floor apparatus in artistic, rhythmic, acrobatic, and aerobic gymnastics

somersault

Full rotation of the body, perfomed in the air

sprung floor

Floor that has springs underneath it. This makes the floor bouncy

straddle

Position in which the legs are stretched wide apart

straight

Position in which the legs are extended, the toes are pointed, and the arms are held at the side of the gymnast or above the head

synchronized

When something is done at the exact same time as something else. For example, when trampolinists compete in pairs, their routines must be completely synchronized, or they will lose points

traceurs

Name for the people who do parkour

trampolining

Disclipine in which athletes perform acrobatic moves while jumping on a trampoline

tuck

Position in which the knees are brought up to the chest

tumbling

Series of gymnastic moves that are performed in a row, without pauses or extra steps between each move

twist

Move in which the entire body twists round in the air

World Championships

International gymnastics competition held most years, but not in years when there's a Summer Olympic Games

Index

A

acrobatic gymnastics 5, 44–45, 53
acrobatics 6, 10
Adilkhanova, Alina 34
aerobic gymnastics 4, 46–47, 53
age 57
Amanar 29
apparatus 11, 15, 17, 20, 22, 25, 29, 31, 35, 41, 44, 47, 50–51, 54
arenas 54
arm strength 13, 24
artistic gymnastics 4, 8–9, 10–33, 53
asymmetric bars 9, 16–17, 18–19

B

back walkover 32–33
backflips 12–13, 29, 31, 48, 57
back somersault with full twist 42–43
balance 4, 8, 21, 23, 33, 34, 44, 45, 46, 47
balance beam 8, 30–31, 32–33
balls 35, 36–37
Beckford, Reiss 23
Belle, David 49
Belyavskiy, David 15
Bevan, Brinn 20
Bhavsar 14
Biles, Simone 16, 31, 38, 56, 57

Biles II 10
Black, Ellie 28
Bretschneider, Andreas 29
Busnari 24

C

cartwheel backflips 12–13
chalk 15
circling 24–25
circus 45
clothing 23, 56
clubs 34, 35
coaching 50
Code of Points 46
college system, American 50
Comăneci, Nadia 39, 56
competitions 54–55
core strength 22
Crete, Minoan 6

D

dance 4, 6, 10, 34, 36, 39, 45
Derwael, Nina 19
Diamidov 15
diet 51
dislocation 20
dismounts 14, 15, 21, 31
Dityatin, Aleksandr 56
double-double dismount 31
double-twisting Kovács 21
Downie, Ellie 17
Drăgulescu 29

E

Egypt, ancient 6
Endo 17

F

facial expressions 45
Fédération Internationale de Gymnastique (FIG) 52
female gymnasts 7
Final Five 8
flair 25
flexibility 4, 10, 26, 33, 46
flips 42, 48
floor 9, 10–11
foam pits 50
food 51
forward entry vault 28
Foucan, Sébastien 49
freerunning 48
Freeman, Jack 15

G

group routines 36–37, 47
Guczoghy 22
gyms 50–51

H

Hamm, Morgan 57
Hamm, Paul 21, 57
Hancharou, Uladzislau 43
hand grips 21, 23

handstand 15, 22, 23, 24, 32
height 56
Hernandez, Laurie 8, 3.
high bar 9, 20–21
high kicks 46
hoops 34, 35, 36–37
horizontal bar see high bar
human pyramid 45

J

Jaeger 16
Jahn, Friedrich Ludwig 7
judges 52–53
jumps 5, 28, 31, 41, 42–43, 46, 48

K

Kabaeva, Alina 39
Kato dismount 14
Khorkina, Svetlana 39
Korbut (move) 31
Korbut, Olga 7
Kovács 21

L

landing the jump 43
leg strength 13
Léotard, Jules 56
leotards 56
lifts 46
Liu Tingting 10

M

Magyar walk 24
mallakhamb 7
Maltese cross 22
medals 55, 56, 57
Melnikova, Angelina 50
mental discipline 49
Mikulak, Sam 14, 55
Miloşovici, Lavinia 53
Minoan civilization 6
Mofokeng, Zama 57
Murakami, Mai 13
mushroom 25
music 10, 46, 57

N

Nemov, Alexei 53
nerves 55
Nonomura, Shogo 22

O

obstacle courses 48
Olympic Games 6, 7, 34, 54
one-armed giant 21
one-handed backflip 57

P

pairs 41, 44, 46, 47
parallel bars 9, 14–15
parkour 5, 48–49
Parkour World Cup 49
perfect scores 53, 56
pike 15, 19, 40
Podkopayeva 10

pommel horse 9, 24–25, 26–27
psychology 51

Q

Quaas, Johanna 57

R

rhythmic gymnastics 5, 34–35, 36–37, 53
ribbons 34, 35
ropes 35
round off 28
rules 52

S

scissor forward 26–27
scoring 52–53, 55
Shaposh 17
Shirai 10
Smith, Louis 24
soldiers 6, 24
somersault 29
Spindle 24
springboard 18, 29
sprinting 28
static strength moves 47
still rings 8–9, 22–23
straight 40
strength 4, 5, 7, 8, 13, 14, 20, 22, 24, 33, 44, 46, 47
supports 10, 11
synchronization 36, 41, 46

T

Tacchelli, Lucia 17
Tanigawa, Wataru 11
teamwork 36–37, 44–45
Thongdee, Chanawit 47
Tippelt 14
Tkachev 16
traceurs 5, 48–49
training 50–51, 57
trampolining 5, 40–41, 42–43, 53
trios 47
Tsukahara 28
tuck 40
Tulloch 22
tumble track 41
tumbling 41

U

Uchimura, Kōhei 38, 55
Ueyama, Yasuhiro 40
uneven bars see asymmetric bars
upper-body strength 18, 26, 38, 47
upstart 18–19

V

vaults 5, 9, 23, 28–29, 48

W

Watanabe, Morinari 52
Whitlock, Max 27
wild parkour 48
World Championships 54
wrist support 11

Y

Yamakasi 49
Yamawaki 22
Yang Bo 31
yoga 7
Yurchenko vault 29

Z

Zhang Jin 30
Zonderland (move) 14
Zonderland, Epke 39, 55

Acknowledgements

DORLING KINDERSLEY would like to thank Helen Peters for compiling the index and Polly Goodman for proofreading.

The publisher would like to thank the following for their kind permission to reproduce their photographs:

(Key: a-above; b-below/bottom; c-centre; f-far; l-left; r-right; t-top)

1 123RF.com: Iaroslav Danylchenko (All Pages). **2 Alamy Stock Photo:** Melissa J. Perenson / Cal Sport Media (cla). **4 123RF.com:** Pattadis Walarput (br). **Getty Images:** Robertus Pudyanto (tr); Jamie Squire (clb). **4-5 Getty Images:** Alex Grimm / Bongarts (bc). **5 Getty Images:** Dirk Waem / AFP (tr); Jamie Squire (tc); PYMCA / Universal Images Group (br). **6 Alamy Stock Photo:** Heritage Image Partnership Ltd (crb). **Dreamstime.com:** Xiaoma (ca). **7 123RF.com:** Pattadis Walarput (tr). **Alamy Stock Photo:** PjrStamps (cra). **Getty Images:** Punit Paranjpe / AFP (clb); Topical Press Agency (tl); John Dominis / The LIFE Picture Collection (bc). **8 123RF.com:** Pattadis Walarput (clb). **Rex by Shutterstock:** Melissa J Perenson / CSM (b). **8-9 Getty Images:** Jamie Squire (c). **9 Getty Images:** Mike Hewitt (c). **10 Getty Images:** Karim Jaafar / AFP (t). **11 123RF.com:** Pattadis Walarput (cl). **Dreamstime.com:** Rodho (cl/Leaves). **Getty Images:** Kiyoshi Ota (b). **13 Alamy Stock Photo:** Yutaka / Aflo Co. Ltd. (br). **14-15 Getty Images:** Jamie Squire. **15 123RF.com:** Pattadis Walarput (clb). **Getty Images:** Naomi Baker (tr); Maddie Meyer (br). **16-17 Alamy Stock Photo:** Matsuo.K / Aflo Co. Ltd.. **17 Alamy Stock Photo:** imageBROKER (tr); Sport In Pictures (cl). **19 Getty Images:** Karim Jaafar / AFP (clb). **20 Alamy Stock Photo:** Amy Sanderson / ZUMA Press. **21 Getty Images:** Alexander Scheuber / Bongarts (tl); Barry Chin / The Boston Globe (cl); Andy Hayt / Sports Illustrated (cr). **22-23 Getty Images:** The Asahi Shimbun (t). **23 123RF.com:** Pattadis Walarput (ca). **Getty Images:** Mark Kolbe (bl); Alex Livesey (tr). **24 123RF.com:** Pattadis Walarput (tr). **Alamy Stock Photo:** YAY Media AS (cra). **24-25 Getty Images:** Alex Livesey. **25 Getty Images:** Dan Mullan (c). **Peter Guyton, All Rights Reserved:** (t). **27 Getty Images:** Naomi Baker (cra). **28 Getty Images:** Naomi Baker (r); Timothy Nwachukwu / NCAA Photos (clb). **29 Getty Images:** Luis Acosta / AFP (br); Matthias Hangst / Bongarts (l). **30 123RF.com:** Pattadis Walarput (c). **Getty Images:** Ulrik Pedersen / NurPhoto. **31 Getty Images:** Jamie Squire (tl, cl, bl). **33 Alamy Stock Photo:** Melissa J. Perenson / Cal Sport Media (cra). **34 123RF.com:** Pattadis Walarput (clb). **Alamy Stock Photo:** imageBROKER (bc). **34-35 Getty Images:** Lillian Suwanrumpha / AFP. **36-37 Getty Images:** Kazuhiro Nogi / AFP. **36 123RF.com:** Pattadis Walarput (cla). **37 Getty Images:** Cris Bouroncle / AFP (tc); Timothy Nwachukwu / NCAA Photos (cb). **38 Getty Images:** Kyodo News Stills (b). **38-39 Getty Images:** Ian MacNicol (tc). **39 Alamy Stock Photo:** Newscom (r). **Getty Images:** Odd Andersen / AFP (tc); Stephen Dunn (c); Minas Panagiotakis (bc). **40 123RF.com:** Pattadis Walarput (br). **Alamy Stock Photo:** Ted Foxx (clb). **Getty Images:** Dean Mouhtaropoulos. **41 Getty Images:** Matthias Hangst / Bongarts (tl); Dean Mouhtaropoulos (br). **43 Getty Images:** Matt Roberts (cr). **44 Getty Images:** Foto Olimpik / NurPhoto. **45 Getty Images:** Dirk Waem / AFP (l); Cem Oksuz / Anadolu Agency (cr). **46 123RF.com:** Pattadis Walarput (clb). **Getty Images:** Matthias Hangst (tr). **46-47 Getty Images:** Robertus Pudyanto. **47 Getty Images:** Robertus Pudyanto (cb). **48-49 Alamy Stock Photo:** Cavan. **48 123RF.com:** Pattadis Walarput (crb). **Alamy Stock Photo:** Elena Vagengeym (bl). **49 Alamy Stock Photo:** Collection Christophel (cr). **Getty Images:** Lucas Barioulet / AFP (tl). **50 123RF.com:** Pattadis Walarput (c). **Alamy Stock Photo:** ZUMA Press (bc). **Getty Images:** Keith Gillett / Icon Sportswire (crb). **50-51 Getty Images:** China Photos (t). **51 Alamy Stock Photo:** ASK Images (crb). **52 Alamy Stock Photo:** Aflo Co. Ltd. (cb). **52-53 Getty Images:** Michael Steele / BEGOC (c). **53 Getty Images:** Adrian Dennis / AFP (c). **Rex by Shutterstock:** John Gaps / AP (tr); Sue Ogrocki / AP (crb). **54-55 Getty Images:** Jamie Schwaberow / NCAA Photos. **54 123RF.com:** Pattadis Walarput (tr). **55 Getty Images:** Kyodo News Stills (tl); Jim McIsaac (tr); Francois Nel (crb). **56 Getty Images:** Hulton Archive (tl); Kyodo News Stills (bl). **57 123RF.com:** Pattadis Walarput (crb/Background). **Alamy Stock Photo:** Waltraud Grubitzsch / dpa picture alliance archive (bl). **Chris Allan Photo:** (cl). **Getty Images:** Matthew Stockman (crb). **58 Getty Images:** Karim Jaafar / AFP (cb). **58-59 Alamy Stock Photo:** PjrStamps (bc). **59 Alamy Stock Photo:** Elena Vagengeym (tr). **Getty Images:** Dirk Waem / AFP (cr); Ulrik Pedersen / NurPhoto (tl); Jamie Squire (bc). **60 Getty Images:** Kiyoshi Ota (tr). **61 Getty Images:** Mike Hewitt (bc). **62 Getty Images:** Robertus Pudyanto (tr). **63 Getty Images:** Dean Mouhtaropoulos (tc). **64 Alamy Stock Photo:** imageBROKER (br).

Cover images: Front: **123RF.com:** Volodymyr Tverdokhlib cra, Pattadis Walarput c/ (Background); **Getty Images:** Karim Jaafar / AFP tc, Naomi Baker br, Francois Nel clb, Ulrik Pedersen / NurPhoto bl, Ezra Shaw c, Jamie Squire tl; Back: **123RF.com:** Volodymyr Tverdokhlib cra, Pattadis Walarput (Background); **Alamy Stock Photo:** Alexander Mitrofanov tl; **Getty Images:** Odd Andersen / AFP cr, The Asahi Shimbun tr, Naomi Baker bl, Dean Mouhtaropoulos cb

All other images © Dorling Kindersley
For further information see www.dkimages.com

Quiz answers

1. B; **2.** C; **3.** A; **4.** B; **5.** B; **6.** 10 cm (4 in); **7.** Parkour; **8.** To learn pommel horse skills; **9.** Every four years; **10.** Acrobatic gymnastics; **11.** The US women's artistic gymnastics team, who won gold in the team event at the 2016 Olympics in Rio. (The team was made up of Simone Biles, Gabby Douglas, Laurie Hernandez, Madison Kocian, and Aly Raisman); **12.** 1936; **13.** Friedrich Ludwig Jahn; **14.** Parallel bars.